In the Mourning Grove

poems by

Susan Auerbach

Finishing Line Press
Georgetown, Kentucky

In the Mourning Grove

*Match days of sorrow with days of joy
equal to the years we have suffered.*
—*Psalm 90*

Copyright © 2024 by Susan Auerbach
ISBN 979-8-88838-784-9 First Edition
All rights reserved under International and Pan-American Copyright Conventions. No part of this book may be reproduced in any manner whatsoever without written permission from the publisher, except in the case of brief quotations embodied in critical articles and reviews.

ACKNOWLEDGMENTS

Thank you to the editors of the following journals where these poems, or earlier versions, first appeared:

Altadena Poetry Review Anthology: "Moving Ground"
Greensboro Review: "Grief Cento"
Gyroscope Review: "Sound Mind"
Last Stanza Poetry Review: "When I Called My Father at 3 a.m."
Please See Me: "Takeaway", "Tending the Shrine, Two Years On"
Spillway: "Appearances"
Versions of "Breathless," "Dreaming Your Name," and "Vanishing Act" appeared in my memoir, *I'll Write Your Name on Every Beach: A Mother's Quest for Comfort, Courage & Clarity After Suicide Loss* (Jessica Kingsley Publishers, 2017).

Thank you, thank you to poets and teachers Dilruba Ahmed, Elline Lipkin, Carla Sameth, and Cathie Sandstrom for encouragement, editing, and helpful suggestions at various stages of this project. Much gratitude also to my family and friends for their loving support in bringing this work to light.

Publisher: Leah Huete de Maines
Editor: Christen Kincaid
Cover Art: Amy Nettleton, AmyNettleton.com
Author Photo: Benjamin Langholz
Cover Design: Elizabeth Maines McCleavy

Order online: www.finishinglinepress.com
also available on amazon.com

Author inquiries and mail orders:
Finishing Line Press
PO Box 1626
Georgetown, Kentucky 40324
USA

Contents

I. Dreaming Your Name

anytime miss wish	1
Moving Ground	2
Dreaming Your Name	3
Descended	4
Takeaway	6
Tending the Shrine, Two Years On	7
Breathless	8
Vanishing Act	9
Cemetery Blues	10
Unpreparedness	11
Here's the Secret:	13
Ripped	15
Grief Cento	16

II. In the Mourning Grove

Beginnings	19
Chill	20
A Whiff, a Trace	21
When I Called My Father at 3 a.m.	22
Snake of the Lake	23
The Undoing	24
In the Mourning Grove	25

III. Means and Ends

Lost Dog	29
Appearances	30
Sound Mind	32
Afterword: Rising Up	33

I. Dreaming Your Name

anytime   miss   wish
       after Gabrielle Calvocoressi

Miss you. Cd fetch you from the airport
anytime, yr tall curly head floating
toward me above the crowd. Tell me all
about New Orleans, Senegal.

Wd love to watch a Japanese film with you.
Even a violent one, just to sit
by you. Maybe rub yr bony shoulders
during. Pick it all apart after.

Miss you sprawled w the dog on the couch.
Chasing chickens, teasing cousins. Fixing
breakfast for yr friends, new ones, old ones,
banter & leap. Wish you could say *miss you* too.

Cd take me sailing finally, heel in high wind—
Mom, you can do it! Meet at kitchen table,
anytime, for a talk, the kind that wonders
through the years. Let me in? Miss this most.

Wd go out to eat w you, anywhere.
Even yr favorite sopping lasts-all-day
chicken burrito at Lucky Boy. You
lucky so long, then not.

Cd hold you when you cry. Hold
my tongue. Bring home help.
Spy you out the window
loping up the drive.

Moving Ground

It was the time when the salamanders
appear underfoot, fresh from their primeval
lairs, their nude red-brown forms lumbering
into the brush with a backward glance.

You dove to catch one, a prize in your palm.
You stared and stroked the gelatinous shape,
awaiting a message from dinosaur time
while hiking your first whineless mile.

Where is that child who stooped to befriend
every worm and lizard in his path?
You stumble into the thicket of your twenties
without a backward glance.

Dreaming Your Name

The name we gave you

we dreamed to see

on a diploma,

a wedding invitation,

maybe someday

in photo bylines

or film credits.

We could picture it

on a Brooklyn doorbell,

a far-flung postcard,

a note of reconciliation.

Never

on a stone.

Never forever

unreachable

in the favorites

on my phone.

Descended

from chicken farmers and garment workers,
our son with his dark teenage Jewfro
could have stepped from a sepia photo.

L'dor va dor, we sang, *from generation to generation.*

We set baskets at his feet, abundant
for the taking—challah and Chelm stories,
plagues acted out at the Passover table.

You shall teach these words diligently to your children.

The wisdom of the ancients beckoned
like dim blue peaks in the distance—
terrain he'd claim, we hoped, with time.

*

When he rent his name from the Book of Life,
we plummeted into a pit
amid the rubble of covenant.

From a narrow place I called out...

Is a child, buried
with the ancestors,
still a descendant?

In this ravaged orchard,
can we ever recover
nectar?

*

God, the soul that you have given me is pure.

Some wear grandfathers'
prayer shawls. I cradle
my son's first prayer book—

the one I inscribed
for his bar mitzvah—
and *open to blessings* I wish

he'd found—the ones I now seize
like rock-climber holds
to claw my way out.

Note: Italicized lines are from Jewish liturgy.

Takeaway

In my dream you
burst out the back door
hellbent on your plan
lay out rope
grab ladder

but you cannot
do this you
vomit
sputter
bolt
from the garage
across the yard

sprung loose
from demons' grip you
heave
shake
spent
cling for hours
to a dim slip
of love still tucked
inside you like an amulet

then hold up your arms
like you did as a child
let me hug you
back to life

you cannot
take away
what I gave you

in my dream.

Tending the Shrine, Two Years On

Sky blue origami cranes
hover in vigil
over your portrait.
Candles stand witness
to the flow and ebb
of your years.

My place is here,
tending the shrine,
warding off the creep of time,
keeping fresh the traces
of your wit, the footprints
of your travels.

I perform my ablutions.
I finger the cold
soapstone heart, kiss
the cracked seashell
and marathon medal.

I dust your album and open
to a boy with a handful
of grasshopper, a grinning teen
atop a sailboat mast, then
a student home for winter break,
gaunt and haunted as a refugee.

When did the end begin?
Like a scrim it shades
every picture,
each moment captured
nearly eclipsed.

Breathless

When grief seizes you, it roars through,
sucks up your breath like a tornado,
spits you out gasping on bare ground.
You strain to recapture your steady
inhale. Like the ring on a carousel
you keep missing it, choking
on bitterness. Like your lost one
you are stalled between worlds, banished
from the flow. You wait for the wild wind
to retreat, the debris to settle.
                    Then one morning,
stillness; you forget you were waiting.
Sweet air seeps in at last—smell, sound,
light—the forward press of time.
The ring lands in your hand.
                    You grasp it,
                            hold on.

Vanishing Act

On your twenty-fifth birthday
I wander the house, kissing your head
in every photo from toothless babe
to troubled man. Those green eyes still blaze
from your high school portrait, tracking mine
in silent entreaty—what? No whiff
of salt hair, no muscled embrace;
only cool glass meets my lips.

From your closet I grab the zip-locked
pack of old T-shirts I saved, sealed
with your scent. I open it fast, breathe
you in, still thick with thrift-store musk,
smoke, sweat. What is the half-life
of a young man's funk? I ration
these releases to last a lifetime.

I walk the beach where you used to surf,
where I used to watch for your silhouette.
But you paddled out too far, dropped over
the beyond. Now I see only other people's sons,
braced and poised against the ocean's pull.

Driving home under mottled clouds,
a rare smudge of rainbow.
                                I'll take it.

Cemetery Blues
after Natasha Trethewey

When they opened up your coffin, your brother let out a wail
Took one look in that coffin, let out a piercing wail
So much love around you but somehow we all had failed

We sat out of view as everyone we knew filed past
Hid behind a curtain as everyone tiptoed past
Still couldn't believe those days had been your last

I couldn't bear to look as they lowered you into the ground
Had to get far away as they lowered you down in the ground
Dirt hitting wood, this world's most lonesome sound

Now all that is left is this little square of earth
Your mark on this world, just a little square of earth
Not a fit home for a boy once filled with mirth

You know I don't belong here, you would have said to me
No way do I belong here, you would have shouted at me
Too many old people underneath the olive trees

Your dad comes to see you, catch you up on all the news
He visits you weekly, fills you in on all the news
Me, what can I do but spill out laments and blues

Unpreparedness

First, says the training manual, *recognize
that an emergency exists.*
                      At a child CPR class,
                      whiplashed back
                      seven years.

Look for unusual behavior, sights, sounds.
                      Him slumped and silent,
                      binging violent movies.
                      When to toggle to high alert?

Use your sixth sense as a parent.
                      What if that's frayed
                      and flailing, untethered
                      from its source?

Be alert for signs that the condition is worsening.
                      Worse, better.
                      Worse still—
                      what he hides.

Decide to take action.
                      Listen to rants,
                      confiscate keys,
                      call doctors but cannot

Obtain consent for help.

Place the person in the recovery position.
                      Homey aroma of roast potatoes.
                      Beacon of Shabbat candleglow.
                      Dog standing by to lick his knee.

                                  *

                            Then that day.
                            Open door.
                                  Feet
                            where no feet
                            should be.

Activate the emergency system.
          Drop phone,
                    bellow
      for help.

Give care until the emergency system takes over.
        Care was all
                we had to give.

Here's the Secret:

let it sit. Let sugars meld
with heated butter; bake it low. With this
my friend Anne won Best Cookie in Fair.

> She had a smiling mom who baked.
> *It's cookie night!* Anne used to crow
> when we were college roommates.

My secret: Start with Anne's recipe
on a stained index card. Beat in the bold
golden yolks of backyard eggs.

> My mother never made cookies; after school
> she was still at school, working. We ate
> Pecan Sandies from a bag. Also:

>> I throw things when I'm mad. Like the time
>> I threw down the keys cursing
>> and my five-year-old jumped, eyes wide.

Check the chip-to-dough ratio; aim
for a crisp sticky mess. Time it so chocolate
wafts through the door for your teens.

> I didn't bake much when they were small;
> I was busy coming late to my vocation.
> We had teddy bear picnics with bananas.

Deliver the goods to their dorm room
or Burning Man camp. Bring enough for friends.
Never too late to be heralded by sweetness.

And if one child should suddenly die,
make dozens for his memorial meal.
Leave a plateful on his unfathomable grave.

Take out cookie sheets on his would-have-been
birthday, whip up could-have-beens
as you stir memory's muddle—

his first flipped crêpe, how he hunched
over the counter crimping pie crust,
his zeal chopping nuts with a fancy knife.

    The time he refused
    to make baguettes with me
    and we never got another chance.

Let it settle.
Some batches
will be salted with tears.

Ripped

Between the unmanned
lifeguard stations
surfers drift and bob like seals
in the swell. Big red lifeboats
lie beached on their sides.

I used to drive you here early
Sundays, after the donut shop,
before the taco place. You
suiting up behind the van
(that rip in the shoulder we never fixed),
eyeing older surfers with cool
nods, trotting fleet-footed
across the sand; me straining
to spot your lean torso in the lineup.

Once the fog was so thick I lost
sight of you before you reached
the break—weak with fear
thank God
you got out quick.

I never saw you catch a wave. Maybe
I missed it. Maybe it was enough
to paddle out and float inside
that briny vast embrace, lulled
by the brightening horizon.

Driving solo five years later,
you came back to claim
that peace, any peace,
but found it
gone.

You got out
quick.

Now I write your name on every beach,
scan the waves for your wake.

Grief Cento

One day it happens, what you have feared all your life:
when you climb to bed you walk
through his blind departure.
Your throat fills with the silt of it.
Next morning you get up and he does not
& the world becomes a bell you crawl inside
& the ringing all you eat—
an obesity of grief.

His absence has gone through you,
hours days weeks months weeks days hours,
like thread through a needle;
now you are fragments on a tailor's floor.

The sea unrelenting wave gray the sea,
turning down through its black water
to the place you cannot breathe.
The little waves with their soft white hands
efface the footprints in the sands;
the shells' empty houses lie scattered.

All things come to an end.
You think you could have stopped it.
How reckless it is,
how careless
that his name is in one pile
and not the other.

You cannot bear his light.

You sometimes go months without remembering him.

Note: Lines quoted and adapted in the tradition of the cento are from: Marie Howe, "How Some of It Happened"; Rita Dove, "The Wake"; Ellen Bass, "The Thing Is"; Philip Larkin, "The Mower"; Nick Flynn, "Sudden"; W.S. Merwin, "Separation"; Donald Hall, "Without"; Stephen Dobyns, "Grief"; David Whyte, "The Well of Grief"; Henry Wadsworth Longfellow, "The Tide Rises, the Tide Falls"; Patricia Fargnoli, "Duties of the Spirit"; Ruth Stone, "Train Ride"; Anne Sexton, "Lament"; Matthew Dickman, "Grief"; David Wojahn, "Written on the Due Date of a Son Never Born"; Laure-Anne Bosselaar, "Stillbirth."

II. In the Mourning Grove

Beginnings

At a white desk in a white bedroom
        my head bends for hours over pencil
and paper, conjuring scribbled worlds.
        Stuffed animals crowd my pillow, awaiting
nightly updates. Nancy Drew mysteries
        stand sentry and muse on the shelves. Whoops
and whines waft in the window from dodgeball
        in the street, summer evening thick
with humidity and cicada thrum.

Plots and characters bubble up
        beneath my fingers, steady and joyous,
too fast for my new loping cursive—
        the sisters' wrong turn in *Lost in a Hurricane*,
The Jackson Twins' capers on camping trips—
        inventing pages of siblings
while others play with theirs till long past dark.

Night swells with crickets, smell of cut grass.
        I stand at the window watching children
drift home. The hushed house, dinner dishes
        settled, my mother retreating to her Chekhov,
my father to his *New Republic*, shadows
        flickering between the furniture.

Here it began: the yearning,
        the learning to be alone,
four summers of stories till I lost
        the map and hurtled, like the girls
in the hurricane, into the eye
        of the storm.

Chill

Ordinary, after-school
afternoon. Unleash
backpack, reach for snack,
see note on table
in father's print:

> *I NEED TO BE ALONE*
> *FOR A WHILE.*
> *YOU CAN CALL ME AT WORK.*

Gut drop. Face flush.
No warning fights
though maybe, lately,
silence. Slip out
of skin. Must call
mother, come
home quick.

Pace house, limbs
on puppet strings.
Half the books,
half the records
and woodblock prints
gone.

Enter mother,
erupts in sobs.
Must hold back
tears, hold her
tight.

> *He hasn't touched me*
> *in two years.*

Feel the chill
that descends
like a shroud.

A Whiff, a Trace

My mother's scent beckons from the front seat
of the Plymouth. Like a cat I hunch forward to nuzzle
the perfumed pillow of her fur collar.

Its feathery nap nestles my cheek;
its musty balm drifts over me like strains
of distant dances. I purr and dream; I am five.

*

In her living room at dusk I ask another question
she will not answer. Her skin, when I dent it
with a kiss, emits traces of hospital hallways.

She stares into nothing, mouth set, head furred
with gray chemo stubble, hands perched
on a belly bloated tight with toxins.

Each week I take her to have it pumped—
quarts of putrid yellow fluid we never
discuss. The doctor thumps her heartily

on the back; she darts him a meek smile
like the one she gave me when I came home
to care for her. Now she cannot meet

my eyes or tell the stories I long
to hear that only a mother knows.
She is 47.

When I Called My Father at 3 a.m.

I'd been shaking for hours. Under all my mother's
blankets I couldn't get warm. I feared

I was dying from the inside out like she
started dying from the feet up the week before,

toes chilled as marble. Who else could I call?
The differences between us could wait.

Six months as live-in cook-companion,
college on hold—now I couldn't breathe

for sobbing, the air still redolent with her flesh,
its soft imprint on the mattress beside me.

Then him by the bed, long-faced, lamp-lit,
hands dangling at his sides. The heat

of his palm on my head, the heft of more blankets,
slow ease of heaves through the shivers.

In the kitchen, light and rattle. Him again,
smiling, aproned, bearing eggs and tea,

the cloying steam of it prickling tears. Him
beside me as I ate, leaning in for an embrace

that had eluded us for years,
now awakened by the call.

Snake of the Lake

    This I can imagine:

my father bolts out of his '78 Corolla
parked at a hasty angle by the boathouse,
leaves the door ajar, the alert bell dinging
over and over in the still middle of the night.
    Alone with pain again, he wrote.
Now he strides down the lake path with his long
shifting gait, pauses by the weeping willow.
He doesn't see the sleeping houses or the ducks
with their wings tucked in on shore.
    He doesn't think of the child he called home,
still closing in on the thousands of miles between us.
He hears only the surge of new meds
in his veins, the siren summons
of the gliding white swan he once dubbed,
in a young man's poem, *snake of the lake*.

    This part I cannot fathom:

him stepping into the cold dark wet
plowing through pillowy silt
till it gives way underfoot letting
the heaviness carry him down down
into the murky softness letting it seep
into clothing nails wrinkles letting
it fill his mouth so he cannot call for help.

    He used to float me around the pool
    in my yellow duck inner tube, hold my hand
    as we waded into waves. I always thought
    he was a swimmer. I always thought—

When he left my mother he left
a note. This time, no note—
only the car with its door flung open,
the blank stare of empty seats, the warning
bell fading into the darkness.

The Undoing

You'd been gone two months
when I started to unravel
the sweater I'd been making for you.
I had no one else to knit for.

       I didn't know you'd come undone.

Was it the dismal dates, the friends
who couldn't come out to play
when you were at loose ends?
Was it me, your undutiful daughter,
too far away for mending?
Or some lapse from long ago
that made you sag and snap?

       The strands I may never unsnarl.

If casting off the ties that bind
is a calling, then you and I
were masters. How I feared the grip
of your ancestral yoke.

What took me months to accrue
took but minutes to undo, the crimped
blue yarn pooling limp in my lap,
spent as I was when I heard the news.

All we ever gave the dead or meant to give
comes back to us—the silly tie, the harsh word,
the cheery airmail letters home:

       I'm learning to knit. What color would you like?

In the Mourning Grove

Groping blind through the valley
of the shadow, I stumbled

on the mourning grove. I must have
heard the tumbling cry of wrens

that echoed my own. My fingers found
the rusty gate, the rough stone walls.

Don't look for me where myrtles grow,
I keened for my mother. The dark hush

of tall cypress, the chill of still waters,
they comforted me as I circled the grove.

I entered its order, took the vow
of remembrance. I searched for signs.

I prayed for companions in my cloister.
It was the cusp of adulthood; few I knew

even hovered at the threshold.
I lay a solitary table.

The grove, my permanent address
when I had no other. I didn't know

I could come and go. I didn't know
that grief is a pilgrimage and the grove

only one of its sanctuaries. Now decades on
when finally many throng the gate,

I welcome them. We can drink together
from the cup. I have been waiting so long.

III. Means and Ends

Lost Dog

Clambering from lap to lap,
    pet to pet, grunt to grunt,
our tiny French bulldog lived

to be held. Held up to sky
    or ceiling by my tall son.
Held over rushing streams

by my husband, bowed legs hanging.
    Scooped up and held by friends,
amazed at her bowling-ball heft.

Held court with bug eyes, bunny ears,
    barrel body. Held back from snapping
at dice or bikes. Held her ground,

all fifteen pounds of it, with Greyhounds,
    even donkeys. Held up traffic
when a driver braked to squeal *is that a Frenchie?!*

Held to my heartbeat like a baby
    at the window, surveying her domain,
purring loud with pleasure.

        Even after the diagnosis,
            held off thinking of the end.
        Held up bits of chicken and croissant

        to her ailing mouth. Held out
            deciding till one too many
    bad days. Held back tears till grown men sobbed.

                For ten years she held
                    our tenderest parts
                in the cup of her paws.

Appearances

1.

The tiny, white-haired woman in the wheelchair
is nearly the last of a diminishing tribe
and I'm here with family to witness
what may be her last appearance.
For years she's spoken at this high school gym
but now she rarely leaves the house and Parkinsons
has swallowed her voice.
         So her daughter tells her story—
from ghetto to cattle car to death camp at 11,
where the women gave her their bread and blankets,
hid her from the guards or held her up
by their shoulders to look older,
fierce handmaids of her survival.
         The tenth graders listening grew up
with tales of *la migra* and border crossings.
They sit stunned by a textbook war made flesh
and a girl their age at war's end, robbed
of childhood and her family of eight. They throng
my husband's aunt for selfies and peek
at her faint blue-gray tattoo, so unlike their own.

2.

I first knew this aunt as a smiling dispenser
of soup and kisses, a champion shopper
in pastel sweater sets, a mom who used to send
her son out to play in perfectly ironed slacks.
Chandeliers and mirrors dwarfed the rooms
of her suburban home; I feared my boys' footprints
on her plush white carpet. Why all the fuss?
I wondered. Until I saw her City Hall debut.
         Pearled and poised at the lectern, blonde hair coiffed,
she spoke softly of attacks by rocks and dogs
en route to school, of barracks' stench and grime
that stuck in her skin. Of how her sister starved
and her emaciated brother lived
to liberation, then died from eating.

    And of her own ritual at Auschwitz:
Each night we'd say goodbye, not good night,
not knowing if we'd live till morning.

3.

Let the gracious woman who emerged
from that terrified child collect porcelain
shepherdesses to tend the pastures of her home.
Let her shop and groom and redecorate.
Let her fashion a haven of luxury
and ease where ordinary days gleam
under crystal ballroom light—
        that no one can ever take away.

Sound Mind

Next time you come, says our dying friend,
bring a chicken. So from the coop
we grab our most ornamental hen,

black and gold cape festooning
regal head, and bear her in a box
to the sickroom.

        Bedside, the potion sits vigil.
        Mira has a date with death
        as the state now allows—no need

        for deceit, just a willing doctor,
        compounding pharmacy,
        the right time when still of sound mind.

Nestled in the quilt, Lulu lifts her wings
in protest, then gurgles as Mira pets
her tawny feathers, smooth as mink.

        How will you know, I ask, *when it's time?*
        Bedside with family on Sunday.
        Grandbabies held out for kisses.

        Is it Thursday? Mira asks, eyelids
        drooping, but it's Monday. She must ration
        every breath to reach her dying day.

Dozing now, friend and hen—
how thin the membrane
at their tender throats.

Afterword: Rising Up
> *after Lucille Clifton*

these   hips are too-big hips, monumental,
off the charts, not made for odes but odious
(pounding at my protrusions in the mirror)
these   hips are my mother's hips, minimized
with pleats and scarves, schooled in the art of deflection
(only *ancient peoples would have worshipped you*)
these   hips were bold birthing nine-pound boys
at home (made for labor, not pigeon pose)—
till mired in the pit of grief (how to get back
on my feet) these hips sprang up to my relief
tore me out of my seat irresistible beat
gotta mourn gotta dance gotta seize this chance
break out rhythms stuck inside nothing left
to hate or hide unleash power swing 'em wide

Susan Auerbach is a retired professor of education who returned in midlife to her first love of creative writing. Her poems have appeared in *Spillway, Gyroscope Review, Greensboro Review,* and other journals, as well as in her memoir, *I'll Write Your Name on Every Beach: A Mother's Quest for Comfort, Courage & Clarity After Suicide Loss* (Jessica Kingsley Publishers, 2017). She blogs at http://afterachildssuicide.blogspot.com and does public speaking on grief, suicide loss, and suicide prevention. She hopes the poems in this chapbook can be a beacon and companion to those who are grieving, as well as an invitation to others to explore—and venture beyond—the mourning grove.

Auerbach is the author of scholarly articles on the role of parents in K-12 education and the editor of *School Leadership for Authentic Family and Community Partnerships: Research Perspectives for Transforming Practice* (Routledge, 2012). Before becoming a professor, she worked as an arts administrator, freelance writer, editor, and education grant writer. In retirement, she led a series of public forums on asylum seekers and a community-based sponsorship effort for an Afghan refugee family. She continues to seek ways to be of use and deepen her Jewish spirituality practice.

Auerbach lives in Altadena, California, where she takes inspiration from the San Gabriel Mountains. When not reading or writing, she enjoys singing, dancing, hiking, traveling, attending arts events, and celebrating with family and friends.

www.ingramcontent.com/pod-product-compliance
Lightning Source LLC
Chambersburg PA
CBHW020220090426
42734CB00008B/1151